# Instant Google Drive Starter

Use Google Drive to safely store and access your files
online in the cloud using your web browser, phone,
or tablet

**Mike Procopio**

PUBLISHING

BIRMINGHAM - MUMBAI

# Instant Google Drive Starter

First published: January 2013


Production Reference: 1220113


Published by Packt Publishing Ltd.
Livery Place
35 Livery Street
Birmingham B3 2PB, UK.

ISBN 978-1-78216-048-9

www.packtpub.com

# Credits

**Author**

Mike Procopio

**Reviewers**

Theodore Chen

Ron Schneider

**Acquisition Editor**

Usha Iyer

**Commissioning Editor**

Meeta Rajani

**Technical Editors**

Worrell Lewis

Priyanka Shah

**Project Coordinator**

Esha Thakker

**Proofreader**

Maria Gould

**Graphics**

Valentina D'silva

Aditi Gajjar

**Production Coordinators**

Aparna Bhagat

Nitesh Thakur

**Cover Work**

Aparna Bhagat

**Cover Image**

Conidon Miranda

# About the author

**Mike Procopio** holds a Ph.D. in Computer Science from the University of Colorado, where he studied Machine Learning and Autonomous Robot Navigation. Mike works as a Senior Software Engineer at Google and lives in Boulder, Colorado with Sharon, his wife. When not slingin' code, Mike can be found running along the trails of Boulder. You can follow Mike on Google+ at `www.googplus.org/mike`, or at `www.mikeprocopio.com`.

Note: The opinions and recommendations stated in this book are Mike Procopio's and not those of Google or his current or previous employers.

I'd like to gratefully acknowledge the support of my wife Sharon while writing this book, and also the broader Google Drive team for giving me the opportunity to be part of such an awesome product!

# About the reviewers

**Theodore Chen** has a degree in Computer Science from the University of Colorado. He has over 10 years of experience writing software for companies such as Sun Microsystems and Parexel. He has worked as a Software Engineer at Google for the last 5 years primarily focused on Google Docs and Google Drive.

**Ron Schneider** has been working in document management and collaboration software for more than 20 years. He is currently a Director of Software Engineering at Google and can be contacted at ron@ronschneider.com.

# www.packtpub.com

## Support files, eBooks, discount offers and more

You might want to visit www.packtpub.com for support files and downloads related to your book.

Did you know that Packt offers eBook versions of every book published, with PDF and ePub files available? You can upgrade to the eBook version at www.packtpub.com and as a print book customer, you are entitled to a discount on the eBook copy. Get in touch with us at service@packtpub.com for more details.

At www.packtpub.com, you can also read a collection of free technical articles, sign up for a range of free newsletters and receive exclusive discounts and offers on Packt books and eBooks.

# packtLib.packtpub.com

Do you need instant solutions to your IT questions? PacktLib is Packt's online digital book library. Here, you can access, read and search across Packt's entire library of books.

## Why Subscribe?

- ✦ Fully searchable across every book published by Packt
- ✦ Copy and paste, print and bookmark content
- ✦ On demand and accessible via web browser

## Free Access for Packt account holders

If you have an account with Packt at www.packtpub.com, you can use this to access PacktLib today and view nine entirely free books. Simply use your login credentials for immediate access.

# Table of Contents

# Instant Google Drive Starter

Welcome to *Instant Google Drive Starter*. This book has been especially created to provide you with all the information that you need to get up to speed with Google Drive, a web-based application that allows you to store, edit, and share your files online using the Internet. You will learn the basics of Google Drive, how to work with files online in the "cloud", and how to share and collaborate in the cloud with other people.

This book is broken down into the following sections:

*So, what is Google Drive?*: Learn about cloud-based storage, how to access your files from anywhere, and why it's so much more convenient than being tied down to using files on just one computer.

*The Google Drive user interface*: Get a high-level overview of all the pieces of the Google Drive user interface. Learn about the files list, Navigation panel, toolbars, search bar, and more.

*Quick start – creating documents and uploading files*: Learn how to create new documents, spreadsheets, and presentations using the built-in programs that come with Google Drive, and how to upload files from your hard drive directly into Google Drive.

*Top 7 features you need to know about*: Learn how to perform tasks with the most important features of Google Drive. By the end of this section you will be able to organize your files, search and filter files, share files with other people, discover and use add-on programs, automatically keep files in sync with your hard drive, and use Google Drive on your phone or tablet computer.

*People and places you should get to know*: Discover the community around Google Drive. This section provides you with many useful links to the project page and forums, as well as a number of helpful articles, tutorials, blogs, and Google+ pages for Google Drive.

# So, what is Google Drive?

**Google Drive** is a place where you can safely store your files online and access them from anywhere. When you use Google Drive, your files are stored remotely on the Web instead of your computer's hard drive. This is the main idea behind "cloud computing".

Once your files are online and "in the cloud", you can access and edit them from wherever you are using any standard web browser. You can even use your smartphone or tablet computer to access your files on the go. You can also share your files with people that you choose, making it easier than ever to collaborate with others and get stuff done.

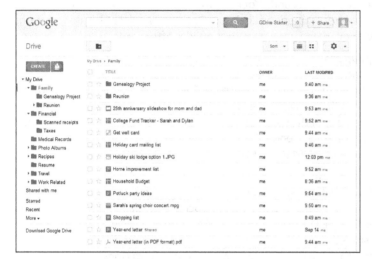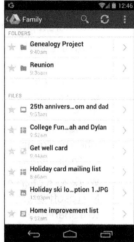

What kind of documents can you keep in Google Drive? Well, everything. You can keep photos, videos, PDFs, text documents, spreadsheets, presentations, and more. Anything that you keep right now on your hard drive, you can store online with Google Drive.

Google Drive also includes an optional free sync program that runs on your computer and keeps files synchronized between a folder on your hard drive and Google Drive on the Web. That way, whenever you create or make changes to a file, either on the Web or on your hard drive, it will automatically be kept in sync between your computer and the cloud.

# What can you do with Google Drive?

Working with files in the cloud is a little bit different from what you may be used to, but it is much more convenient. You can edit your files from anywhere and you can share and collaborate on files with other people. Importantly, your files in the cloud are safe if there is ever a problem with your hard drive. Here are some examples to give you an idea of the things you can do with Google Drive:

✦ **Create a presentation**: Let's say you need to make a presentation. You create a new **Google Slides** presentation in Google Drive, get a rough draft of the slides in a reasonable shape, and share it with your co-worker. (With Google Drive, there is no need to e-mail versions of files around.) Your co-worker makes a few comments on your slides, and you make the recommended changes. Once you've given the presentation, you share it publicly so everyone has access to the slides afterwards.

✦ **Write a report as a group project**: Your teacher or boss has tasked you with creating a report for a work or school project. The data is collected in a **Google Sheets** spreadsheet, with each person in the team adding their own data. They can even enter data using their phone or tablet, and with Google Drive, everyone can edit the spreadsheet at the same time—there is only one copy of the spreadsheet to keep up to date. Next, the entire team collaborates on the report, using Google Docs, with each person writing a section. And when you're done, you can convert it to a PDF file and share it with your boss or teacher for their review.

✦ **Work with Microsoft Office documents**: Let's say a company that you work with uses Microsoft Office, and sends you a Microsoft Word document. You upload the document to a shared folder on Google Drive, where you and a co-worker review it and make a few changes to the shared copy. When done, you e-mail the revised version back to the person who sent it to you as an attachment, all directly from Google Drive.

✦ **Upload and share vacation videos**: You just got back from vacation, and are eager to share videos of you learning to ski with your family. The videos are too large to e-mail. So instead you upload the videos from your camera's memory card into a new folder in Google Drive, and then share that folder with a few of your family members. They get an e-mail notification, click on the link in the folder, and are able to enjoy the moment when you got up on two skis for the first time. They can view the videos and photos right on their phone or tablet.

✦ **Keep a backup of your important files**: You have several years of irreplaceable family photos, school projects, and home business records stored on your computer's hard drive. Because hard drives can fail, you want to back these files up. So you download and install the Google Drive sync program, which then automatically uploads and syncs files and folders of your choice to the cloud. If something ever happens to your computer, your cloud backup is there for you in Google Drive.

As you can see, with Google Drive, you aren't limited to just built-in document types (such as Google documents, spreadsheets, and presentations). You can open, view, share, and comment on almost every type of file such as PDFs, Microsoft Office files, photos, and videos. And with third-party add-on programs, you can go beyond viewing and actually edit special types of files such as Microsoft Office documents, all online from any web browser, phone, or tablet computer.

## First steps for using Google Drive

Getting started with Google Drive is easy and free. All you need is a Google account and an Internet connection. You may already have a Google account (for example, an e-mail address ending in gmail.com), and if not, creating one is easy. Note that you can use any e-mail address, not just those ending with gmail.com for your Google account.

To get started, simply visit Google Drive on the Web with your web browser at https://drive.google.com/. From there, you can log in with your existing Google account or create a new one.

You don't have to make the switch to the cloud all at once. You can start using Google Drive for creating new documents here and there, or you can upload files one at a time as you need them in the cloud. Alternatively, download the sync program to automatically keep large amounts of folders and files in sync between your computer and Google Drive. Whether a little or a lot, it's up to you how much you use Google Drive.

# The Google Drive user interface

The Google Drive **user interface (UI)** is the screen you see when you visit the main Google Drive page with your web browser (located at `https://drive.google.com`). It's made up of seven main sections and looks something like the following screenshot:

Note that 3 – Context menu only appears when right-clicking on a file.

**Heads up: The Google Drive user interface will change over time!**

Google makes continual improvements and adds new features to its products in response to customer feedback. As a result, the user interface shown previously will change and evolve over time, so what you see online may not exactly match the screenshot given.

Here is an overview of each section, corresponding to the preceding numbered screenshot.

# 1 – Files list

The **Files list** is the main list where your documents and other files show up. It is generally similar to how files are displayed on your computer, except with Google Drive your files are in the cloud.

| My Drive ▸ Family ▸ **Reunion** | | |
|---|---|---|
| ☐    TITLE | OWNER | LAST EDITED BY ME |
| ☐  ☆  📷 Reunion Photos | me | 1:00 pm |
| ☐  ☆  Lodge Confirmation Receipt.pdf | me | 1:09 pm |
| ☐  ☆  Reunion Attendee List | me | 1:00 pm |
| ☐  ☆  Reunion Email #1 | me | 1:00 pm |
| ✔  ☆  Reunion location.jpg | me | 1:09 pm |
| ☐  ☆  Reunion Slideshow | me | 12:54 pm |

Here are some important notes on the Files list:

✦ Each file is displayed in a row showing its filename and an icon. The icon shows what type of file it is: text document, image, PDF folder, and so on.

✦ To open a file, simply click on its name.

✦ You can select multiple files by using the checkboxes on the left-hand side. Many actions, such as starring and sharing, can apply to multiple files.

✦ You can star (or "mark") a file by clicking on the star icon, which is your way of saying this file is "special". Later, you can use the **Navigation panel** (discussed later) to show only starred files.

✦ One or more labels can appear next to the file's name. If the file is in a folder, the name of the folder will be shown. If the file is currently shared with one or more people, the label **Shared** will appear.

✦ To the right of the filename is a column called **OWNER**. This shows who owns the file, which is generally whoever created it. If you created the file, this will say **me**. If someone else created the file and shared it with you, it will show their name instead.

✦ A date will appear on the end of the row. Depending on how you've chosen to sort your Files list, the date can represent the date the file was last modified or the date the file was last opened by you, and so on.

✦ On any row, you can right-click with your mouse to bring up the Context menu, which shows some advanced actions you can perform on files. Refer to the *Context menu* section given later for more information.

Now that you've got your files in front of you, it's time to start working with them. Read on to learn about the toolbars and the Context menu.

## 2 – Toolbars

The **toolbars** give you quick, one-click access to several important features, with additional actions you can take appearing under the **More** button. The following toolbar appears when you have selected a document:

Here are the file actions you can access from the toolbar:

✦ **1 – Share**: Opens up the Share window that lets you share a file with one or more people. Refer to the *Sharing files with other people* section given in the *Top features you'll want to know about* section for a tutorial on sharing in Google Drive.

✦ **2 – Organize**: Opens up the **Organize** window that lets you choose the folder in which you want to put a file.

✦ **3 – Remove**: Puts the document into "Trash" if you own it, or prevents it from appearing in Google Drive if it is shared with you.

✦ **4 – Preview**: Opens up the **Preview** panel with a side bar that appears on the right-hand side that contains additional details about a file (refer to the Preview panel screenshot given next).

✦ **5 – More**: Displays a menu containing additional actions that you can take on the selected file. This is the same menu that appears if you right-click on a file to display the Context menu (described in the following section).

To the right-hand side of the main toolbar is a second toolbar with additional options:

✦ **1 – Sort menu**: Lets you choose how your Files list is sorted. You can sort it by:

   ° **Last edited by me**: When you last made a change to the file

   ° **Last modified**: When the last change to the file was made by anyone, including you and people with whom you have shared the file

   ° **Last opened by me**: When you last viewed or opened the file

   ° **Title**: Alphabetically by the name of the file

   ° **Quota used**: By the amount of space the file is taking up in Google Drive

✦ **2 – View type**: Controls whether your Files list shows up as a row-by-row listing (in the list format, as shown throughout this book), or in a grid of larger images but with less detailed information.

✦ **3 – Settings menu**: Displays a menu containing settings (configuration options) for Google Drive, as well as **Help** information, **Keyboard shortcuts**, and other options.

## 3 – Context menu

The **Context menu** appears when you use the mouse to right-click on a file in the Files list. The menu also appears when you click the **More** button on the toolbar.

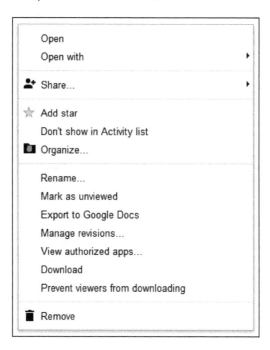

This menu gives you access to all the actions you can take on a selected file. Here's a quick description of some of the most important actions:

- ✦ **Open**: This option opens the file in a new browser tab. This is the same as simply clicking on the file.

- ✦ **Open with**: This option lets you choose a specific application to use to open the file. For example, this could be an add-on program that you previously installed (refer to the *Using third-party add-on applications* section given in the *Top features you'll want to know about* section).

- ✦ **Share...**:This option opens up the sharing screen where you can share a file with one or more people (refer to the *Sharing files with other people* section given in the *Top features you'll want to know about* section).

- ✦ **Add star**: This option marks the document with a star.

- ✦ **Don't show in Activity list**: This option prevents this item from being tracked and showing updates when you are in the **Activity** mode.

- ✦ **Organize...**: This option opens the **Organize** screen, where you can choose which folder to put the selected file in.

- ✦ **Rename...**: This option allows you to type in a new name for a file.

- ✦ **Mark as unviewed**: When a file changes in Google Drive, it appears in bold, indicating it has not been viewed since the last time it was changed. Select this option to manually toggle whether the file should be marked as unviewed.

- ✦ **Manage revisions**: This option opens the **Manage revisions** screen, allowing you to view and download previous versions of a file, as well as upload new versions.

- ✦ **View authorized apps...**: This option opens the **Authorized apps** screen, showing which third-party add-on applications have permission to access the selected file.

- ✦ **Make a copy**: This option creates a copy of the file in Google Drive.

- ✦ **Download**: This option downloads the selected file to your computer's hard drive.

- ✦ **Prevent viewers from downloading**: If you own the file (if it was created by you), this option will appear and selecting it will prevent people you have shared the file with from downloading a copy to their computer.

- ✦ **Remove**: This option puts the document into the Trash if you own it, or prevents it from appearing in Google Drive otherwise if it was shared with you. Refer to the *Deleting files* section given in the *Top features you'll want to know about* section.

# 4 – Navigation panel

The **Navigation panel** appears on the left-hand side of the screen, and serves two main purposes. First, under **My Drive**, your personal system of folders will appear. This is the folder hierarchy or tree that you may have created (or not—the choice is yours!). Think of it as a filing system that you use to keep your files organized.

Secondly, the Navigation panel lets you quickly change "views" of your files. For example, you can click on **Starred** and only those items that you have starred will appear in the Files list.

Using the Navigation panel is very easy:

+ Click on any folder to show the files in that folder.
+ Reorganize folders by dragging-and-dropping them where you like (for example, under a different folder).
+ Put files in a folder by dragging the files from the Files list into the folder of your choice.
+ Star a file by dragging it from the Files list onto the **Starred** label.
+ Put a file in **Trash** by dragging it from the Files list onto the **Trash** label.

There are many items in the Navigation panel that you can click on that will change the "view" of your Files list. (Note that some labels are initially hidden underneath the **More** label.) Here are some of the labels you can click on, and what they do:

✦ **My Drive**: This is where all the files you create are stored. Click on the small arrow to the left-hand side of **My Drive** (or, you can double-click on the **My Drive** label) to expand this root folder and to see all of the folders underneath it.

✦ **Shared with me**: This is where files and folders that were created by someone else, but have been shared with you, appear.

✦ **Starred**: This will show only those files that you have previously **Starred**.

✦ **Recent**: This lists all the files that have recently been edited or opened by you. It's an effective way to get to your most frequently used files.

✦ **Activity**: The **Activity** view lists all files, in order of the most recently modified, as well as information about who last modified the file. It's a useful view when collaborating with others on a group of documents. For example, in the workplace or in a school setting, use this view when multiple people may be making changes to documents shared with the larger group.

✦ **Offline Docs**: Lists those files that are available for you to view offline without an Internet connection. If you don't have this feature enabled, clicking this will give you details on how to enable it. Offline Docs are supported only when using the Google Chrome web browser.

✦ **All items**: Shows a listing of all the files in your Drive, no matter what folder you created them in or whether they're shared with you. If you're sure you have a file but can't find it, use this view (also useful in conjunction with the Sort function).

✦ **Trash**: When you choose to remove a file that you created (via the **Remove** option in the toolbar or the Context menu), the file will be placed in the Trash. Use the Trash view to see all files that are in your Trash. For more information, refer to the *Deleting Files* section given in the *Top features you'll want to know about, 1 – Working with files and folders* section.

✦ **Owner, type, more**: This opens up an advanced search options pop up that allows you to search for files using a variety of criteria, such as file type. For more information, refer to the *Searching for files* section given in the *Top features you'll want to know about* section.

✦ **Download Google Drive**: This section takes you to a page where you can download the Google Drive sync program to your computer, which will keep files in sync automatically between Google Drive and your computer. Refer to the *Using the Google Drive sync program* section given in the *Top features you'll want to know about* section.

# 5 – Preview panel

The **Preview panel** appears on the right-hand side of the screen and shows you additional details about a selected file. Note that the Preview panel is not shown by default. To show it, first select a file, and then click on the **Details** icon in the toolbar.

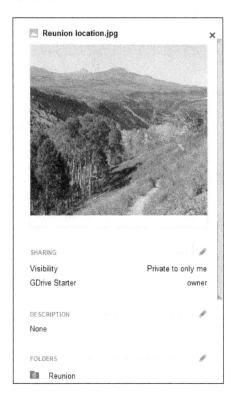

Here's an overview of the information shown about a file when the Preview panel is open:

✦ **Filename**: The name of the file appears at the top. Click on the filename to open the file.

✦ **Thumbnail**: If available, a small picture or thumbnail will be shown for the file.

✦ **Sharing**: This option lists the owner of the file, and all the people who have access to a file. If you created the file, the owner will be you, and the people with whom you have shared the file will each be listed here.

✦ **Description**: Every file can have a description, which you can provide. To add or update the description, simply click on the current description text and start editing.

✦ **Folders**: This option shows the folder in which a file appears.

✦ **Revisions**: This option shows the previous versions that have been recorded for a file.

✦ **General Info**: Information about when a file was last modified, and by whom, will appear here.

# 6 – Search bar

The **search bar** appears at the top of the screen in Google Drive:

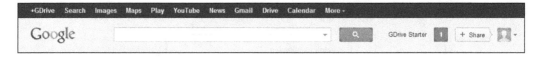

It contains several key parts such as:

✦ **Links to other Google Properties**: At the very top are links giving you one-click access to several of the most prominent Google services such as **Search, Images, Maps, Gmail, Google+,** and more. These will open in a new tab when you click on them.

✦ **Search box**: Type in a search query in the search box to search for files in Google Drive that contain the specified text. Refer to the *Searching for files* section given in the *Top features you'll want to know about* section for more information on searching.

✦ **Account information and Google+**: This shows you information about the currently logged in user (you), allowing you to switch accounts or sign out as needed. This is also where you can share to Google+, and also check your Google+ notifications.

# 7 – Create and upload buttons

The **CREATE** and upload buttons appear on the left-hand side just above the Navigation panel, and are the starting point for creating new documents and files in Google Drive.

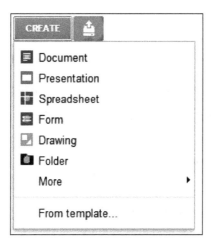

Clicking on the **CREATE** button will display a menu that allows you to choose the type of file you would like to create. To the right-hand side of the **CREATE** button is the upload button, which you use to upload files from your computer's hard drive directly into Google Drive. The following section shows you how to use these buttons to create new files in Google Drive.

# Quick start – creating content in Google Drive

By now you've gotten up to speed on the basics of cloud computing and the Google Drive user interface. You've also seen that Google Drive lets you store files online, so you can view and edit them from anywhere. But how do your files get there in the first place?

There are three ways you can get your files into Google Drive. First, you can use the built-in applications to create new files such as documents and spreadsheets. Second, you can upload files and folders from your hard drive directly into Google Drive. As a third option, you can also install the Google Drive sync program on your computer, which will keep files in sync automatically between your hard drive and Google Drive.

## Creating new documents with the built-in applications

Google Drive comes with a built-in set of office productivity applications that work in the cloud, right out of the box. No need to install them; they're automatically there and ready to go.

There are four main programs included in Google Drive: Docs (for documents), Sheets (for spreadsheets), Slides (for presentations), and Drawings.

✦ **Google Docs** is a word processing program that lets you create and edit text documents. There is full support for text formatting, images, lists, tables, and styles.

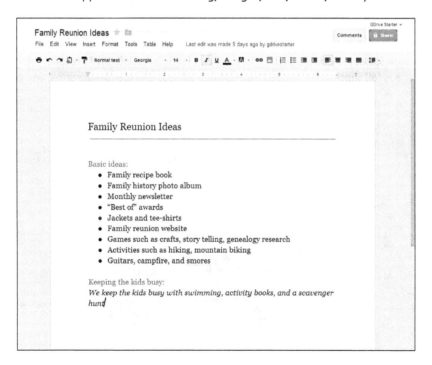

✦ **Google Sheets** is a spreadsheet program that lets you organize information in a tabular format. There is full support for formulas, sorting, charting, multiple worksheets, cell formatting, and pivot tables.

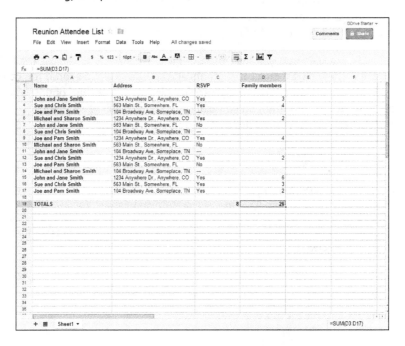

✦ **Google Slides** is a presentation program that lets you create and present graphical slides. There is full support for images, formatting, tables, themes, animations, and projecting.

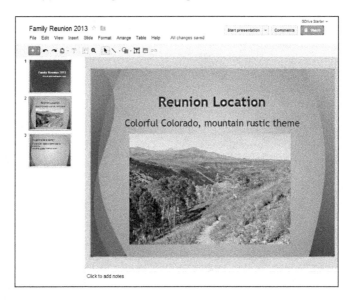

✦ **Google Drawings** is a graphics program that lets you create visually rich graphics including flowcharts and other diagrams. There is full support for shapes, text, images, layout, and ordering.

All of the built-in Google Drive programs support both printing and exporting to PDF and Microsoft Office formats. Each program also has full support for sharing, so you can share any file created with any of these programs with anyone (or keep them private so that only you can see them).

## Creating a document

To create a document using one of these programs, first click on the **CREATE** button, and then choose the document type you wish to create from the menu that appears:

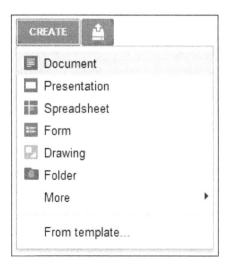

For this example, we will create a document, which represents a text document created with Google Docs (the built-in word processor program).

 When you create a new document, it will always be placed into the current folder.

After choosing the new document type to create, a new tab will open up in your web browser, and the selected Google Drive program will load. By default, your document will be named **Untitled document** as shown in the upper-left corner of the screen.

After clicking on the name textbox, you can type in a new name for your document:

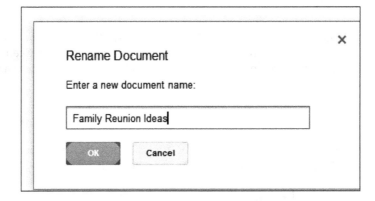

## Working with your new document

From here, you can start typing into your new document. You can insert images and tables, change text formatting, and define and apply styles—all the things you expect to be able to do in a word processing program. The same applies to using the other built-in programs including spreadsheets, presentations, and drawings.

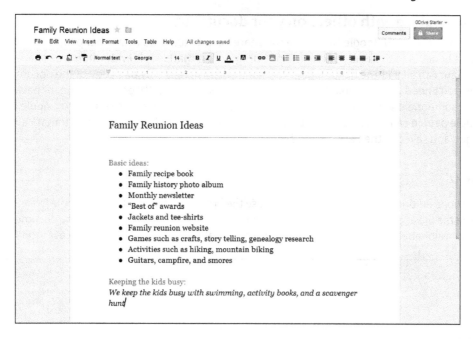

There are many things you usually do in Google Drive (using the toolbar and the Context menu) that, if you prefer, you can do from inside the Google Docs, Sheets, or Slides program. We've just seen how you can rename your document, but you can also share, star, organize, add comments, and print. For example, starring and organizing can be done with the icons to the right-hand side of the filename, and sharing can be accessed under the **File** menu or by clicking the **Share** button in the upper-right corner.

## Saving your data with the built-in applications

When using any of the built-in Google Drive programs, there is no need to manually click on **Save**. Instead, saving is automatic and happens continuously in the background, while you type.

 Although documents made with the Google Drive programs show up in your Files list, they do not count against your storage space in Google Drive, no matter how big they get.

## Collaborating with others on your document

We've seen that with Google Drive, you can share your documents with other people. One of the biggest benefits of the built-in Google Drive programs is that people with whom you share that document can all edit the document *at the same time*. There is only one copy of the document, so we don't need to worry about e-mailing revisions back and forth, or overwriting, or having to merge someone else's changes. With the real-time collaboration feature built into Google Drive, multiple people can edit a document simultaneously and their changes are all automatically merged and saved in the background as they type.

## Working with your new document in Google Drive

When done editing your document, simply close the browser tab and return to Google Drive. You will see the file appear in the Files list. Depending on what **Sort** you have chosen, the document will appear in alphabetical order (when sorting by **Title**) or at the top (when sorting by **Last modified**).

Here are just some of the things you can do with your newly created document (for more information refer to the *3 – Context menu* section and the *2 – Toolbars* section given in the *The Google Drive user interface* section):

✦ **Open** it for viewing or editing by clicking its name in the Files list.

✦ **Share** it with one or more people by selecting the document and clicking on the **Share** icon in the toolbar.

✦ **E-mail** it as an attachment to one or more people by right-clicking on it and choosing **Share** and then **Email as attachment** from the Context menu. (Because this may make an unwanted copy of the file, it is often better to share the document directly instead.)

✦ **Rename** it by right-clicking on the file and selecting **Rename** from the context menu.

✦ Place it into a different folder by dragging-and-dropping it into the appropriate folder in the Navigation panel, or by selecting the document and clicking on the **Organize** icon on the toolbar.

✦ **Download** the file in PDF format by choosing **Download...** in the Context menu and selecting **PDF** as the desired format.

✦ View additional details by selecting it and clicking on the **Preview** icon on the toolbar.

✦ Remove it (put it in **Trash**) by selecting the document and clicking on the **Remove** icon from the toolbar.

## Uploading files from your computer

Another way to get files into Google Drive is by uploading them from your computer's hard drive. This is a great way to quickly move files or folders to the cloud as you need them. Once in the cloud, you can share your files with anyone (or keep them private so that only you can see them), and access them from anywhere.

**Heads up: Windows, Mac, and Linux may look a bit different**

In the examples in this section, we have used Microsoft Windows. If using Mac or Linux, the screens for choosing the files or folders to upload will look a little different. In all cases, though, the basic functionality is the same.

### Example – uploading individual files

Let's run through a quick example for uploading individual files.

1. First, open the Upload menu by clicking on the upload button in the upper-left corner, and then select **Files...**:

2. Next, you will be presented with a screen that lets you choose which files to upload:

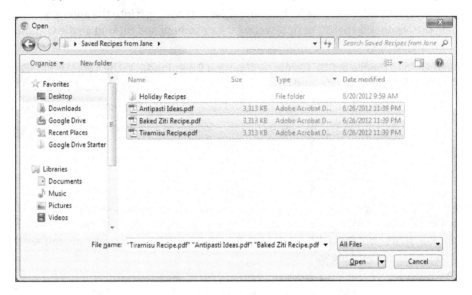

3. Select the file you wish to upload. You can also select multiple files to upload using the *Ctrl* or *Command* key. Then click on **Open**.

4. At this point, your upload will begin, and could take anywhere from a few seconds, or minutes, or more to upload depending on how large the file is and how fast your Internet connection is.

Read on to learn how to monitor the progress of your file upload.

## The upload progress window

Once your upload has started, a pop-up window will appear in the bottom-right side of the Google Drive user interface, called the **upload progress window**.

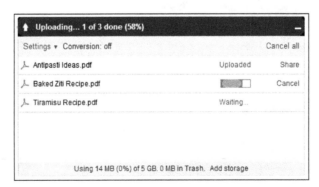

Using this pop-up window, you can:

✦ **Watch** as each file is uploaded, one at a time. A file's individual progress is shown with a progress bar, and the overall progress is noted at the top of the pop up.

✦ **Cancel** a file's upload (if it has not yet completed uploading) by clicking on **Cancel** next to the file in question. You can also cancel the entire upload with the **Cancel all** button.

✦ **Open** a file by clicking on its name (available once it has completed uploading).

✦ **Share** a file with other people by clicking on **Share** next to the file you want to share (available once it has completed uploading).

✦ **Monitor** the amount of storage space that you have in Google Drive, and the amount that you are using (this information appears at the bottom). Refer to the *Managing your storage in Google Drive* section within the *Uploading files from your computer* section for more information.

## Uploading files using drag-and-drop

You can also upload files using drag-and-drop, which is the easiest way to upload files. To do so, simply select one or more files on your computer, drag them into the Files list area of the Google Drive user interface, and drop (release the mouse button).

This will start your upload just as if you had selected the files using the upload menu, and you'll be able to monitor the upload with the upload progress window described previously.

## The upload settings menu

You can set certain upload-related options using the upload settings menu. This menu is accessed by clicking on **Settings** in the top-left corner of the upload pop up:

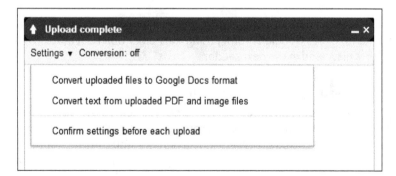

There are three main options in this menu:

- ✦ **Convert uploaded files to Google Docs format**: If selected, then certain file formats such as Microsoft Office files will be converted to their corresponding Google type (document, spreadsheet, or presentation). File conversion applies mainly to converting Microsoft Office files into the corresponding Google type. So, Microsoft Word files turn into Google Docs documents, Microsoft Excel files turn into Google Sheets spreadsheets, and Microsoft PowerPoint files turn into Google Slides presentations. Once converted, those files get all the same benefits as if they were created with a Google program in the cloud, including collaborative editing (where multiple people can edit the file at the same time).

- ✦ **Convert text from uploaded PDF and image files**: If selected, then **Optical Character Recognition (OCR)** technology will be applied to any PDF files or images that are uploaded. Any text found in the PDF or image will be extracted and placed in a Google Docs document, along with a snapshot of the original image or PDF.

- ✦ **Confirm settings before each upload**: If selected, before each upload you will be shown a screen that lets you choose which of the previously mentioned options to apply to just that one particular upload. For example, you may want to convert certain files to Google format, but not others. In this case, you would leave this feature off, but ask to confirm settings before each upload so you could enable conversion for just that one upload.

## Uploading folders

In addition to individual files, you can also upload entire folders at once. This is a great way to upload large amounts of files into Google Drive with just a few clicks. When you upload a folder, all "subfolders" within that folder, and all folders within each subfolder, and so on are uploaded.

Note that uploading folders works a little differently when using Google Chrome versus other browsers. This example uses Google Chrome; using the Folder Upload feature in Firefox and Internet Explorer is discussed in the next section.

**Heads up: Uploading large folders can take a long time!**

Depending on the size of the folder you select, and the sizes and number of files and folders contained in the selected folder, your upload could take several hours or more. You can monitor the upload progress using the upload pop up to see how the upload is going and how long it will take.

To upload a folder, follow the ensuing steps:

1.  First, open the upload menu by clicking on the upload button in the top-left corner, and then select **Folder...**:

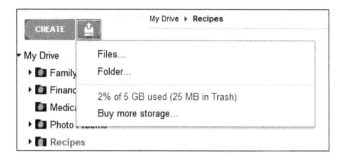

2.  Next, you will be presented with a screen that will let you choose what folder to upload:

3. Select the folder to open (you can only choose one folder to upload at a time) and click on **OK**. At this point the upload progress window will appear in the lower-right corner, and your upload will begin:

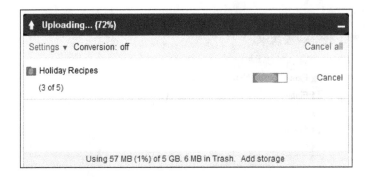

4. From here you can monitor the progress of the upload and perform other upload-related functions. For example, you can cancel the folder upload while it is in progress (cancelling does not remove files in the folder that have already been uploaded).

5. When complete, you can share the uploaded folder with one or more people using the **Share** button, or navigate directly to the folder by clicking on its name.

## Enabling folder upload with Firefox or Internet Explorer

Google's Chrome web browser lets you upload folders without the need to take any extra steps. If you use Firefox or Internet Explorer, however, you will have to enable a special Java applet or plugin in order to upload folders.

To enable folder upload for Firefox or Internet Explorer:

1. Open the upload menu by clicking on the upload button on the upper-left side, and then select the **Enable folder upload...** option:

2. Next, you will be presented with a screen asking you to confirm enabling the folder upload. (Alternatively, you can download the Chrome web browser, which doesn't require the special Java plugin):

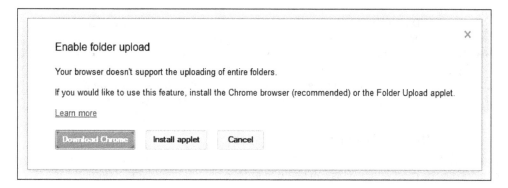

3. After clicking on **Install applet**, you may be prompted by your computer with a security warning about the applet, prompting you to confirm the installation of the Java plugin.

4. Once the applet is installed, you can then return to the upload menu and select the **Files and folders...** option.

5. Finally, select the folder you wish to upload, and the upload will proceed as described here.

## Managing your storage in Google Drive

In Google Drive, just like on your hard drive, you have a certain amount of space that you can use for storing files. You get a fixed amount of storage for free, and you can purchase additional storage at any point in time.

The amount of storage you're using, and the total amount of storage you have available can be seen in the upload menu:

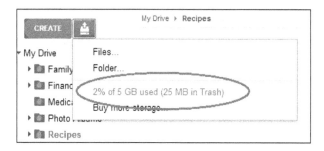

This storage information is also displayed at the bottom of the Navigation panel.

This shows you how much space you have available in Google Drive, and how much of it you're currently using. If you have reached your storage limit, you will not be able to upload files. Purchasing more storage can be done with the **Buy more storage...** link.

 Documents created with built-in Google programs (Docs, Sheets, Slides, and so on) do not take up any storage space, nor do files that other people have shared with you. Files you've uploaded, however, do count towards your storage. Uploaded files also include files automatically synchronized with your computer; refer to the *Using the Google Drive sync program* section given in the *Top features you'll want to know about* section.

### Viewing files that are taking up the most space

If you are close to running out of space, you can quickly find files stored in Google Drive that are taking up the most space. This can be done as follows:

1.  Select **All Items** in the Navigation panel on the left-hand side (you may have to expand the Navigation panel by selecting the **More** option).

2.  In the toolbar, select the **Sort** button and select **Quota used**.

3.  The files taking up the most space will appear at the top.

From here, you could then delete any unnecessary files, freeing up storage space.

## Uploading files with the Google Drive sync program

A third way to get files into Google Drive is to install the optional Google Drive sync program for PC or Mac. This will automatically keep files in a special Google Drive folder on your hard drive in sync with your files in the cloud in Google Drive. It's a great way to quickly and reliably get large amounts of data on your hard drive into the cloud. For more information, refer to *Using the Google Drive sync program*, the fifth feature in the following section.

# Top 7 features you need to know about

So far, we've covered the basics on how to use Google Drive including navigating the user interface, creating new documents, and uploading files. As you start to use Google Drive day-to-day, you'll see there is much more you can do with it. This section will teach you about some of the most common tasks and important features in Google Drive.

## 1 – Working with files and folders

Google Drive is your place to access and organize your files in the cloud. Just like with your regular computer, you can open and edit your files. You can also create a "filing system" where everything is kept in a system of organized folders.

### Opening and downloading files

Viewing, editing, or downloading your files in Google Drive is only a click away. Here's a quick overview:

+ **Open a file**: To open a file, simply click on its name. The file will open in a new browser tab. Depending on the type of file, you can edit it (in the case of a Google file), or you can get a preview of it using the built-in viewer program.

+ **Open a file with a specific application**: If you have add-on applications installed that can work with a particular file, you can choose to use the application to open a particular file. Right-click on the file, and choose **Open with** from the Context menu. Then choose the application you want to use to open the file. The file will open in a new browser tab using the selected application. For more information, refer to the *Using third-party add-on applications* section given later in this section.

+ **Download files or folders**: You can download any file in Google Drive by selecting one or more files, right-clicking, and choosing the **Download** option. For Google Docs, Sheets, and Slides files, you'll be asked to choose what format to download the file in (PDF, Microsoft Excel, and so on). For other files, choosing this option will download the actual file. You can also download entire folders. And if you'd like to automatically keep an always-current copy of the files in Google Drive on your hard drive, you can do that, too (refer to the *Using the Google Drive sync program* section given later in this section).

## Previewing files

The Google Drive Viewer is a built-in program that offers a rich preview when opening files that are not Google documents, spreadsheets, or presentations. For example, images, videos, and PDF files will all be opened with the Google Drive Viewer.

In addition to offering a rich preview of your photo, video, PDF, or other file types the Google Drive Viewer also gives you access to many of the functions you normally do in Google Drive. For example, using the **File** menu at the top, you can share, rename, star, organize, download, and edit the description of your file. You can even add comments to a file for you and people with whom you've shared the file with to see.

## Creating a new folder

With Google Drive, you can create folder structure that can be as simple or elaborate as you like. The following steps will show you how to create a new folder:

1.  To create a new folder, click on the **New folder** button in the toolbar.

New folder

2. You'll be asked to give your new folder a name, and once you've typed in a name, click on the blue **Create** button.

3. After creating the folder, you'll be taken directly to it in Google Drive. From here, you can create new documents or upload files directly into this folder.

## Moving a file into a folder

You can also move existing files into a particular folder. There are two main ways to move files into folders. You can use the **Organize** screen, or you can use drag-and-drop. To use the **Organize** screen:

1. First, select one or more files or folders. (You can use the *Ctrl* or *Command* key to select more than one file or folder.)

2. Bring up the **Organize** screen by clicking on the **Organize** toolbar button at the top, or by right-clicking and selecting **Organize...** from the Context menu. The **Organize** screen will appear as follows:

3. Note that the **Organize** screen shows you where the selected file currently is (in this example, under **Genealogy Project**). From here, you can select where you'd like the file to be instead.

4. Identify the folder location you want the file to be in, and then click just to the left-hand side of the folder icon. A checkmark will appear, indicating that is where the file will be. In this example, we have chosen a different folder under **Family** called **Reunion**.

5. Click the blue **Apply changes** button.

6. A notification will be displayed telling you that the files have been moved to the folder you specified.

An even simpler option compared to using the **Organize** screen is using drag-and-drop to move your files into folders. To move one or more files into folders using drag-and-drop:

1. Select one or more files or folders.

2. Click on one of the selected files.

3. Drag the files over to the Navigation panel on the left-hand side of the screen, hovering the mouse over **My Drive**.

4. **My Drive** will expand automatically showing you folders underneath it.

5. Once you've found the folder where you'd like the files to go, release the mouse, which will "drop" the files into the desired folder.

6. A notification will be displayed telling you that the files have been moved.

# Deleting files

Sometimes, you'll be done with a file and will no longer want it in Google Drive. Fortunately, deleting one or more files from Google Drive is easy. To do so:

1. Select one or more files or folders in your Files list. (You can use the *Ctrl* or *Command* key to select more than one file or folder.)

2. Click on the **Remove** icon in the toolbar, or right-click and select **Remove** from the Context menu.

3. A notification will be displayed telling you that the files have been moved to the **Trash** (see *The Trash* section, next ).

 You can only delete files that you own.

# The Trash

The **Trash** is a special folder where files that you remove from Google Drive first go before they are permanently deleted. It's basically a holding area where removed files go to ensure you can easily restore a file in case you accidentally delete it.

To see what's in the Trash, go to the Navigation panel, and click on **Trash**. You may have to expand the navigation panel by clicking on the **More** option. Files and folders that have been put into the `Trash` folder will appear here.

From the `Trash` folder, you can do several important things including the following:

✦ **Permanently delete a file**: To permanently delete one or more files from the `Trash` folder, first select the file or files you want to delete. Then, click on the **Delete forever** toolbar button at the top, or right-click on the selected files and select the **Delete forever** option from the Context menu. Note that you cannot undo deleting a file from the trash—once it's deleted, it's gone, and it cannot be recovered.

✦ **Delete all files from the Trash folder**: To permanently delete all files from the Trash, click on the **Empty trash** toolbar button at the top. You will be prompted to confirm if you want to permanently delete all files from **Trash**. Again, this action cannot be undone—once the trash is emptied, the deleted files cannot be recovered.

✦ **Restore a file**: If you change your mind and decide you want a file back, it is easy to restore a file from the `Trash` folder to its original location (where it was before you removed it). To do so, select the file and click on the **Restore** toolbar button (or you can right-click and select **Restore from trash** from the Context menu). The file will be taken out of **Trash** and placed back into its original location.

As you can see, the `Trash` folder is a useful place or "holding area" where files go before they are fully deleted. Note the importance of the terminology here: *removing* a file from Google Drive refers to moving it into the `Trash` folder, which can be undone (by restoring it). *Deleting* a file can only be done from the Trash, and deleting is a permanent operation. You cannot get deleted files back.

### Deleting shared files

There are two important things to keep in mind when deleting shared files:

✦ **For files that you own,** but are shared with others, removing them will result in those files no longer being shared. Since sharing a file doesn't make a copy, but instead actually gives access to the original file, deleting a file that you have shared with others means that those people will no longer be able to access it (unless they made a separate copy of it for themselves).

✦ **For files that were shared with you,** you are not the owner, and so you cannot delete those files. You can only delete files that you own. Yet, you may still be done with those files, and want them out of Google Drive. In this case, you can still remove them by selecting them and selecting **Remove** from the toolbar or the Context menu. However, this will not delete the file, and the owner of the file (or person who shared it with you) will not be notified. Instead, it will simply prevent the file from showing up in Google Drive.

## 2 – Searching for files

Google Drive includes a powerful search function. Searching lets you quickly find your files based on one or more criteria that you specify. There are two main ways to find files in Google Drive: searching with text, and searching with predefined criteria known as **filters**. In both cases, searching takes place in the search bar:

### Searching with keywords

You can perform a *full text* search by searching for one or more words. When you run such a search, results are returned based on one or more of your search terms matching any of the three fields given next:

1. The title of the file.

2. The text content of the file, which could be text from a PDF file, a spreadsheet, words in a Google Docs document, and so on.

3. The description of the file (which you can set or view in the Preview panel).

To start searching, simply type in your search keyword in the search box. In this example, we're searching for the keyword **holiday**. As you type, note that some search results will pop up instantly underneath your search query. These "instant results" represent only a partial set of search results. Often, what you're looking for will pop up in the "instant results", and you can then click on an item to open it directly.

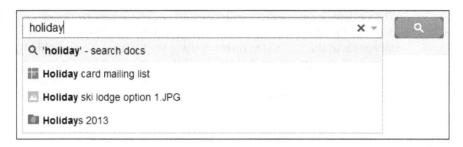

To fully run your search and see *all* search results, type in your search query and then press *Enter* or click on the blue search button on the right-hand side. This will perform a full search, returning results based on not only the file's title, but also the text content of that file.

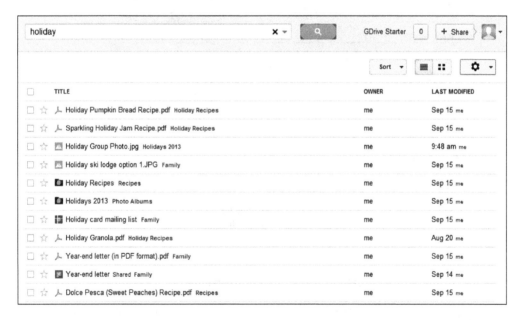

In this example, searching for **holiday** returned matches based on both the filename and the file's text contents. For example, the word **holiday** appears in the text of the Google Docs document **Year-end letter,** and so it shows up in the search results. Note that text from PDF files is also searchable.

From these search results, you can open the resulting file by clicking on it. You can also perform any other functions you're used to by selecting the document and using the toolbar, or by right-clicking the file to bring up the Context menu.

**Sorting your search results**

When you perform a search, search results will come back by default sorted by **Relevance**. This means that the most relevant search results will appear at the top, based on how strong the match is. If you would like to sort your search results instead by the last time the file was modified, you can do that as well by choosing **Last modified** from the **Sort** menu in the toolbar.

## Searching with filters

Another way to search for files is to use one or more predefined criteria, called **filters**. To get started, first open the **advanced search options** by clicking on the small arrow in the right-hand side of the search box (circled in the following screenshot):

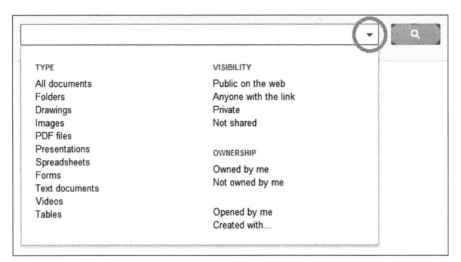

Here are some of the general categories of things you can filter by:

✦ **Type**: Use this category to filter by file type. For example, you can show only PDF files, folders, images, and all of the various Google types (documents, spreadsheets, presentations, and drawings).

✦ **Visibility**: Choose one of the options here to show files based on their sharing status. For example, you can choose **Private**, which will show files that are still private to you (not shared broadly), but which may be shared with one or more people. For more information, refer to the *Visibility Options* sections given in the *Sharing files with other people* section.

✦ **Ownership**: This category filter can help you quickly find files for which you either are or are not the owner. For example, you can choose **Owned by me** to show all files for which you are the owner, thereby excluding files that have been shared with you (for which you are not the owner).

✦ **Other**: There are some other useful miscellaneous filters you can use. Choose **Opened by me** to show all files that you have ever opened, and **Created with...** to show files that were created with a particular third-party application (if you have such applications installed).

As an example, let's say you want to see a list of all your PDF files in Google Drive. Simply open up the advanced search options, and choose PDF files. A small filter chip will appear to indicate the criteria that you're filtering on (here, PDF files), and the matching search results will be shown. In this example, the search results are all PDF files in Google Drive (no matter what folder they're in):

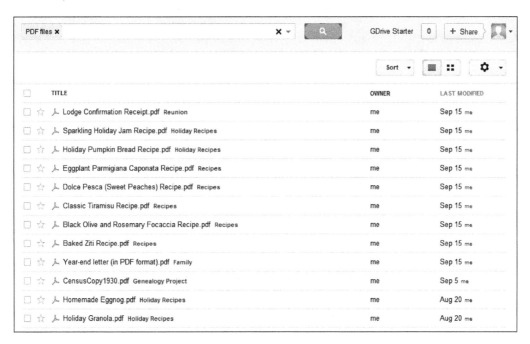

From here, you can select and perform specific file operations on one of your search results. Or if you are done, you can click on the **X** in the search box to clear the search results and return to where you were.

## Combination searches

You can also search by keyword and one or more filters, all at the same time. First, select one or more filters in the advanced search options. In this example, we have selected **Images**. This will return all the images in Google Drive.

You can further narrow down these results by searching by keyword. Simply type in your search query to the right of the existing chip (here, it says **Images**). In this example we have searched for **naiya**. This combination search will show you all images that have the word **naiya** in the title. (Note that searches are not case-sensitive.)

With the ability to search by keyword, filter criteria, or a combination of both, you should have no trouble quickly finding files that you're looking for in Google Drive.

## Searching by people

Searching for files shared with you by another person is easy in Google Drive. Simply type in the user's name or e-mail address, and their name will appear in the drop-down list of "instant" results shown previously. Click on their name, and this will search for all files in Google Drive shared with you by that person.

## 3 – Sharing files with other people

One of biggest benefits of storing your files in the cloud is how easy it is to share them with other people. No more e-mailing files around. Instead, with a few clicks you can give other people access to your file, right in the cloud. You don't need to make a separate copy, because all collaborators receive access to the exact same file. And if you assign edit permissions, those people can also edit the file, with the changes showing up immediately in Google Drive. Collaborating with others has never been easier.

By default, all files you create in Google Drive are not shared. They are private to only you, and only you can see them. This applies to both uploaded files, files created with the built-in applications, and files uploaded from your hard drive using the optional sync program. In situations where you want to collaborate with others on a file, that's where sharing comes in.

## The Sharing settings screen

The **Sharing settings** screen is where you can view and change all sharing permissions associated with a file that you own. To open the **Sharing settings** screen, select one or more files or folders, and then click on the **Share** button in the toolbar.

> **Sharing a file from a Google program**
>
> The built-in Google programs (Docs, Sheets, Slides, and Drawings) as well as the Google Drive Viewer all let you share from directly within the program. In each program, simply click on the **Share...** option from the **File** menu at the top.

The **Sharing settings** screen has seven main parts, given as follows:

✦ **1 – Link to share**: Paste this link into an e-mail or a chat message to let recipients access the document directly. (To copy the link, select the text, right-click, and choose **Copy**.)

✦ **2 – Share link via service**: Click on the Gmail, Google+, Facebook, or Twitter icons to automatically share a link to this document via the selected service.

✦ 3 – **Who has access (visibility)**: Click on the **Change** link to be able to set the visibility options to keep the file private, shared via a link, or shared publicly. Refer to the *Visibility Options* section given in the following section.

✦ 4 – **Sharing recipient list**: People with whom the file is currently shared will appear in this list. Refer to the *The sharing recipient list* section next.

✦ 5 – **New sharing recipient field**: Type in one or more e-mail addresses in this field to add people to the sharing recipient list. Here is where you also set the level of sharing permission to assign to the new recipients (**Can edit**, **Can view**, and so on). Refer to the *Sharing access levels (permissions)* section given later in this book.

✦ 6 – **Messaging options**: By default, when you share a file with someone, they will be notified via e-mail. This is helpful for the sharing recipients because they will have a record of the shared file in their e-mail with a link that they can refer to in the future. Uncheck the **Notify people via email** checkbox if you do not want this e-mail to be sent (for example, you could just send them the link directly yourself). Optionally, you can also specify a message by clicking on **Add message**. It is often helpful to do so, because you can give some background information on the file and why you're sharing it. Your note will show up in the sharing e-mail sent to the recipients.

✦ 7 – **E-mail options**: Check the appropriate checkbox if you would like to send a copy of the sharing e-mail to yourself (useful to see exactly what your sharing recipients will see, and to confirm that your e-mail went through). You can also indicate to paste the contents of the file in the e-mail, so recipients can preview the document directly from their e-mail.

## The sharing recipient list

The sharing recipient list shows all the people with whom the file is currently shared. In this example, the owner is listed, and there is one other sharing recipient. Note that you can share the file with as many people as you like.

Each sharing recipient is associated with a level of access (**Can view**, **Can comment**, or **Can edit**). For more information refer to the *Sharing access levels (permissions)* section given next.

To remove someone from the sharing recipient list, click on the **X** button on the right-hand side of their entry, and then click on the blue **Apply changes** button. This will remove that person's access to the file (unless it is shared publicly). You can change someone's access level in a similar way. Note that the person whose access you change or remove will not be notified (they will not receive an e-mail).

**Sharing with groups**

You can even share the file with Google Group e-mail lists, which will share the file with everyone in that group. This is especially useful in work, family, or educational settings where group membership will change over time.

## Sharing access levels (permissions)

Every time you add a sharing recipient, you also indicate a *sharing permission*, or level of access that a person will have to the file being shared. There are four main access levels that a person can have for a particular file:

✦ **Viewer** (shown as **Can view**): A viewer can open the file, read and see its contents, but cannot make any changes. They cannot delete the file and they cannot share it with other people.

✦ **Commenter** (shown as **Can comment**): A commenter can do all the things that a viewer can with the file, and they can also leave comments in certain types of Google files. They cannot otherwise change the file, and like viewers, they cannot delete the file or share it with other people.

✦ **Editor** (shown as **Can edit**): An editor can do all the things that a viewer or commenter can with the file. In addition, they can also make changes to the file, and, unless you specify otherwise, they can share it with other people. Editors cannot delete files shared with them; only the owner can do that.

✦ **Owner** (shown as **Is owner**): An owner is generally the person who created or uploaded the file. An owner has full permission to a file, so they can edit the file and share the file with other people. The owner is also the only one who can delete the file.

Just as you can assign these sharing permissions to people, on files that are shared with you by someone else, you will have your own access level specified for the file—view, comment, or full edit permissions.

## Visibility options

Every file has one single level of visibility that applies to the file broadly, regardless of specific individuals with whom you have shared the file. By default, this visibility level is **Private**, and only specific people who you have shared the file with can access it. But if you like, you can change this to be more widely shared.

To change the overall visibility of a file, click on the **Change...** link to the right-hand side of the first entry under **Who has access** in the **Sharing settings** screen. This will bring up the **Visibility options** screen as shown in the following screenshot:

There are three main visibility options you can choose from:

✦ **Private**: The file is private and visible only to you and to the people with whom you explicitly share the file. These people will each appear as sharing recipients in the **Who has access** section. If they're not listed here, they don't have access. Use this option when you only want certain people to be able to access your file.

✦ **Anyone with the link**: Anyone who has received the link to this file can access it. The link to the file is the "Link to share" at the top of the **Sharing settings** screen, and this link is initially made available only to you. Anyone who you send this link to will be able to access the file. This is a good option to choose when you want the file to be easily accessed by a large number of people; for example, you could send the link out to an e-mail list for a group project.

✦ **Public on the Web**: Anyone on the Internet can find and access the file. The file can show up in search results, and anyone who knows the Web address of the file will be able to access it. Choose this setting when you want your file to be discoverable and accessible by everyone. They do not need to be signed into a Google account. This is a good option if you want to publish the link to your file on a website and have everyone easily access the file.

If you choose **Private**, you will be able to specify the access level (permission) for each person. If you choose either **Anyone with the link** or **Public on the Web**, you can also choose the access level, but it will apply to anyone accessing the document with those two visibility options. For example, you may want to give viewing permissions to anyone on the Web using the **Public on the Web** option. In this case, you could also give editing permissions to specific additional people with whom you explicitly share the file in the sharing recipients list.

# Example – sharing a file

Basic file sharing is simple and can be done with just a few steps:

1. Open the **Sharing settings** screen by selecting one or more files to share, and clicking on **Share** from the toolbar or the right-click context menu.

2. Type in the name of one or more recipients to share the file with.

3. Choose a level of access (permission) for the sharing recipients. Choose from **Can view**, **Can comment**, or **Can edit**.

4. Click on **Add message** and type in a short personalized message.

5. If desired, check the **Send a copy to myself** box which will also e-mail you about the file you just shared.

6. Click on **Share & save**.

At this point, an e-mail will be sent to each of the newly added sharing recipients, with your message and a link to the document.

Your sharing recipient will click on the link in the e-mail they receive, and your file will be opened in their web browser. If they have edit permissions, they can edit the file, too. The file will also show up in the **Shared with me** section of their Google Drive for easy later reference. They can also find the shared file by going back into their e-mail.

You can change sharing settings at any time by selecting the file and opening the **Sharing settings** screen. For example, you could remove somebody from the sharing recipients list, and this would mean that person could no longer access the file. You could also simply change their access level; for example, somebody may e-mail you requesting permissions to edit a file that they only have view permissions for, and you could grant them in this way.

That's it for basic sharing! It only takes a few seconds to collaborating in the cloud.

## Sharing a folder

Sharing a folder is a popular and effective way to share multiple files at once. This is especially helpful when you're collaborating on a project as a team. In this case, all of the project's documents and files (text documents, spreadsheets, photos, PDFs, and so on) are all in the project folder, and the entire team receives access to that folder and the files inside.

This works well because when you share a folder, all of the files in that folder receive the same sharing permissions as the parent folder. And importantly, all new files that get created or uploaded into that folder also receive the same permissions. That means that if you share a folder with editing permissions with other people, any new content that gets created in that folder is automatically editable by everyone with whom the folder is shared.

### Files other people share with you

Just as you can share files with other people, other people can share files with you. You can quickly find files other people have shared with you by clicking on the **Shared with me** option in the Navigation panel. All files that have been shared with you will show up here, and you can then work with them just like you can with any other file, depending on your permissions (refer to the *Sharing access levels (permissions)* sections given previously).

If you like, you can also move these into your main Google Drive folder (**My Drive**) by dragging-and-dropping the file onto the **My Drive** label. (You can also select the file and use the **Organize** screen.) This doesn't change the fact that the file is shared with you, but it does make it a little more convenient to access.

## 4 – Updating your settings

Google Drive includes some preferences that you can optionally set. Usually, the defaults work just fine, but if you'd like to tinker a bit, you can do so in the **Settings** page. To get started with settings, click on the "Settings" icon in the toolbar on the upper-right side, which will show the Settings menu:

From here, you can choose from several options:

+ **Display density**: Choose from among three separate options that will control how much information can fit inside the Google Drive window at one time. This refers to the "compactness" of the user interface.

+ **Settings**: Opens up a screen with additional settings including your default language, time zone, and some user interface preferences.

✦ **Upload settings**: Expand this submenu to set options related to uploading files. Refer to the *The Upload settings menu* section given previously.

✦ **Manage apps**: Choose this option to display a screen that will allow you to manage your installed applications. Refer to the *Using third-party add-on applications* section next.

✦ **Keyboard shortcuts**: This option will pop open a handy quick-reference list of keyboard shortcuts that you can use to quickly access your favorite commands.

✦ **Help**: Takes you to the main support page where you can find detailed information on all of the features in Google Drive.

# 5 – Using third-party add-on applications

As you've seen, Google Drive offers a useful set of built-in applications that let you create and edit documents, spreadsheets, presentations, and drawings. With third-party add-on programs called Drive Apps, you can extend the functionality of Google Drive to do even more.

These Drive Apps read, write, and edit files stored directly in Google Drive, so you can use them to do useful things with your files all on the Web. And just like the built-in programs, you can use Drive Apps from anywhere (including your phone or tablet) and then share the files you create with them with other people.

## What can you do with Drive Apps?

From faxing and making diagrams, to project planning and editing video, the possibilities with Drive Apps range far and wide. Here is a list of some of the popular third-party applications that work with Google Drive that you can install and start using right now:

✦ Send and receive faxes directly from/to Google Drive with **HelloFax**. You can fax PDFs, images, Microsoft Office files, even Google Docs documents. Go to www.hellofax.com.

✦ Make visually sharp diagrams and flowcharts with **LucidChart**. Go to www.lucidchart.com.

✦ Create 2D and 3D floor layouts and building designs with **FloorPlanner**. Go to www.floorplanner.com.

✦ Edit, crop, resize, and style photos with **Aviary**. Go to www.aviary.com.

✦ Manage and schedule your next project with **Gantter**. Go to www.gantter.com.

✦ Edit videos and make movies in the cloud with **WeVideo**. Go to www.wevideo.com.

✦ Make your own music with **UJAM**. Go to www.ujam.com.

✦ Create stunning slide presentations with **SlideRocket**. Go to www.sliderocket.com.

✦ Create and edit Microsoft Office documents, spreadsheets, and presentations natively with **InstallFree Nexus**. Go to nexus.installfree.com.

✦ Create mind maps and brainstorming diagrams with **MindMeister**. Go to www.mindmeister.com.

## Installing Drive Apps

**Drive Apps** are similar to other programs on your computer, in that you have to first install them before you can use them. However, there is a very important difference: with regular programs, you're installing an actual copy of the program on your hard drive, and you can access it only from your computer.

With Drive Apps, however, you're adding it to Google Drive, online and in the cloud. Nothing is actually installed on your computer's hard drive. What's great about this is that just like you can access Google Drive from anywhere, you can access your Drive Apps from anywhere, too. Everything is online and in the cloud—files and programs.

Installing Drive Apps is done via the Chrome Web Store and takes just a few clicks. But note that you don't have to use Chrome to use Drive Apps; they can be used from any web browser such as Firefox or Internet Explorer, in addition to Chrome.

To install a Drive App, follow the ensuing steps:

1. Visit the Chrome Web Store by navigating your web browser to `https://chrome.google.com/webstore`. (You can also click on **Get more apps** in the Manage Apps screen; refer to **Managing your installed Drive Apps**.)

2. Click on the **Collections** label on the left-hand side of the screen. This will expand a list of collections from which you can choose. From this list, click on **Google Drive**.

3. A list of available Drive Apps will now appear, looking something like the following screenshot (the actual apps that appear may be different). As you can see, there is a large variety of apps to choose from.

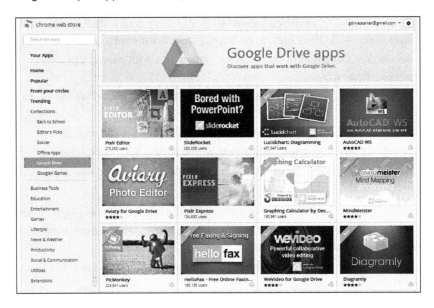

4. To get more details about an app, simply click on the app's picture. A details pop up will appear. We've clicked on **Aviary Photo Editor,** as shown in the following screenshot:

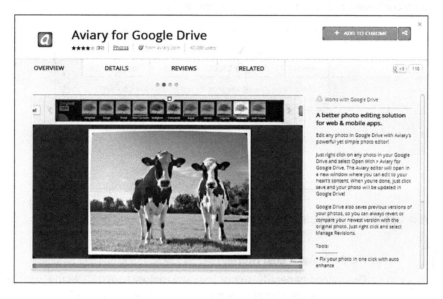

5. From here, you can read about an app and see screenshots of it in action. You can also read reviews and rate the app. Importantly, this pop up is where you actually install the app.

6. When you're ready to install the app, click on the blue **ADD TO CHROME** button, and accept the confirmation prompt that appears, as follows:

7. At this point, the Drive App is now installed. Returning to Google Drive, you will need to refresh your browser (using *F5* or the reload or refresh option), and you'll get a confirmation that the app has been installed:

That's it! Your app is now installed and ready to use.

**Do Drive Apps cost money?**

Drive Apps generally do not cost any money to install. Many Drive Apps are completely free to use, while others are free but occasionally display advertisements in the user interface. Still others are free to use for a while on a trial basis, but you must then pay for a license to use the app after the trial period.

### Choosing to use an application by default

For many apps, you will have the option to use the app by default. Checking this box means that when you click on a file in Google Drive to open it, if the particular Drive App is able to open the file, then it will always be used to open the file. Specifically, it will be used instead of the Google Drive Viewer (which is the default app otherwise).

In other words, the Drive App that you've chosen to use by default will now be used to open files of types it can open. This is generally desirable, because while the Google Drive Viewer can only preview files, Drive Apps generally let you edit the files.

Note that you can always use any program, not just the default program, to open a particular file. To do so, right-click on the file and choose the desired application from the **Open with** option in the Context menu.

## Using Drive Apps

Using Drive Apps in Google Drive is just a matter of a few clicks. There are two main ways you can use Drive Apps. First, you can create a new file; many, but not all, Drive Apps support this. Second, you can open an existing file with a particular Drive App.

## Creating a new file with a Drive App

If a particular Drive App is able to create new files, it will show up in the **Create** menu, which you use to launch the app.

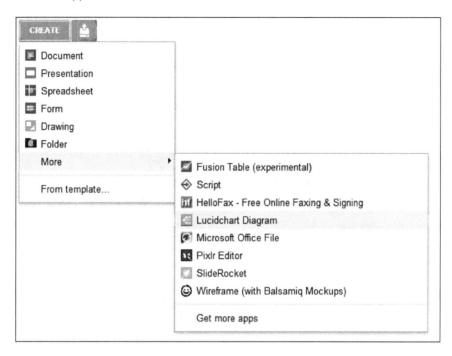

To create a new file using a Drive App:

1.  Click on the red **CREATE** button in the upper-left corner to open the Create menu.
2.  Click on the **More** option, appearing towards the bottom of the Create menu. This will pop open a submenu of Drive Apps that you've installed with which you can create new files. In this example, we see a number of apps.
3.  Choose the app with which you want to create a new file
4.  Your selected app will load in a new browser tab, and then you're ready to start using the app.

From here, the exact way the application works will vary depending on the app. Generally, you'll edit your new file in the app's user interface, saving it when done. Where does the file go when you save it? Back into Google Drive, where you can then edit it again, download it to your hard drive, or even share it with other people.

## Opening an existing file with a Drive App

The other main way you can use a Drive App is by selecting one or more files, and then selecting the Drive App you'd like to use to open that file.

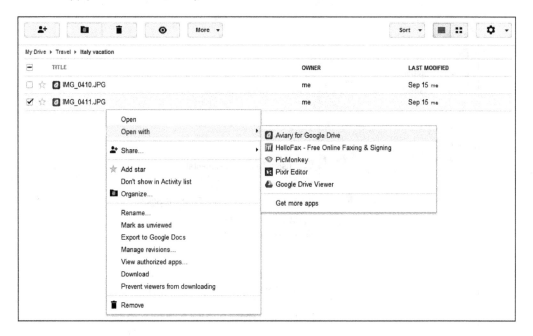

To open an existing file with a Drive App:

1. First, select a file, and then right-click on the file to bring up the Context menu (you can also select the file and click on the **More** toolbar button).

2. From here, select the **Open with** option that will show you a list of Drive Apps that you have installed that are able to open the file you selected.

3. In this example, we clicked on an image, and there are several apps installed that can open photos, including **Aviary for Google Drive** which we just installed.

4. Choose the app you'd like to use to open the file. The app will load in a new browser tab, and the selected file will appear, ready for action. Here, we have chosen to open the file in Aviary, one of many photo editors available that work with Google Drive.

5. When done, save the file in the app, and the changes will be written back to the file in Google Drive.

It's that simple! Just a few clicks and you're up and running with your newly installed Drive App.

## Security permissions

Drive Apps are subject to very strict security requirements. Importantly, before apps can read or write files in Google Drive, you must first explicitly authorize them to do so. The first time you use a particular Drive App, whether with the **Create** or **Open** scenarios described in the previous section, you will be shown a special security screen by Google:

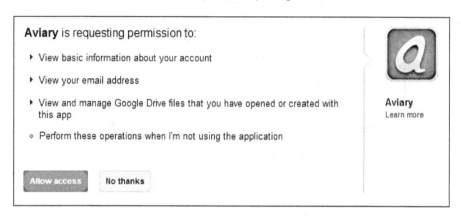

This screen lists the types of things the particular Drive App is requesting your permission to be able to do. It will only be able to function if you grant these permissions.

In this example, the application is requesting four types of permissions, such as the ability to read basic account information including your name and e-mail address. It is also requesting to be able to write files into Google Drive. Finally, it is requesting permission to read files that the application created, or that you have previously used the application to open. This means that the app cannot just go accessing any file in Google Drive—only ones it created, or you previously opened with the app.

To grant these permissions to the app, click on the blue **Allow access** button, and the app will be allowed to proceed. Otherwise, click on **No thanks** and this will prevent the application from having any access to Google Drive (and it will not be able to run).

## Managing your installed Drive Apps

To see a list of Drive Apps that are currently installed in Google Drive, choose the **Manage apps** option in the **Settings** menu by clicking on the Settings button on the toolbar. This will pop up the **Manage apps** screen:

The **Manage Apps** screen lists all applications that have been added to Google Drive. This screen is also a convenient point to find and install more Drive Apps, just click on the **Get more apps** link at the top.

### Drive App options

There are several actions you can perform related to a Drive App. To see these options, first open the **Manage apps** screen shown previously, and then click on the **Options** button next to the app you're interested in. A special options menu will appear:

Here's an overview of some of these options.

+ **View product page**: Choose this option to open up the app details pop up described earlier, which will show important details about the app such as the app description, screenshots, company website, support information, and reviews.

+ **View all files this app is authorized to access**: In most cases, applications request permission to be able to access only those files that it created, or that you specifically choose to open with the app. Refer to the preceding *Security permissions* section. Choose this option to list all of those files that the application has permission to read and edit.

+ **View all files this app created**: Choose this option to see a list of all the files that the application has created in Google Drive. Generally, this will be all files that you saved after using the **CREATE** button, but in some cases, applications may also write files into Google Drive in other situations.

+ **Remove this app**: Choose this option to uninstall the Drive App from Google Drive.

## Uninstalling a Drive App

When you choose **Remove this app** from the **Manage apps** screen for an app, this action will completely uninstall the application from Google Drive. In particular:

+ The app will be fully removed (uninstalled). It will no longer appear in the Create menu or the Open With menu.

+ You will not be able to create new files with the uninstalled app or open existing files with it.

+ Any files you created with the app that appears in Google Drive will not be removed. In other words, if you create a file with a Drive App, it will stay in Google Drive even after uninstalling the app. Uninstalling does not remove files, it only removes the app.

+ Because Drive Apps live in the cloud just like your files, removing an app from Google Drive means this change will be reflected regardless of where you access Google Drive (assuming you're using the same account, of course). Uninstalling a Drive app does not affect the current computer or mobile device you're working from.

+ Some apps create proprietary file formats that can only be read by the app. If you uninstall one of these apps, then you may not be able to open files you created earlier with it, even though those files are still in Google Drive.

+ You can always reinstall an application again later after uninstalling it.

# 6 – Using the Google Drive sync program

Google Drive comes with an optional but popular sync program available for download for PC and Mac. The main purpose of this program is to keep your files in sync between Google Drive on the Web and a special `Google Drive` folder on your computer's hard drive—all automatically and in the background.

Keeping files in sync in this way brings you many benefits:

✦ **Access your files anywhere**: Your entire set of files in Google Drive is available on the Web (at `https://drive.google.com`), and also on your PC or Mac (in a folder on your computer's hard drive called `Google Drive`).

✦ **Make changes anywhere**: Your files are always up-to-date no matter where you make changes. If you make a change in one place, the file is updated everywhere else: in Google Drive on the Web, in the `Google Drive` folder on your computer's hard drive, and on your mobile device (if you have the Google Drive app). Updates are all done automatically.

✦ **Keep a backup of your important files**: Cloud storage is an excellent backup option, because your files are kept safely in the cloud. You have a safe, "off-site" copy of your important data that will be there in the event your computer encounters problems.

✦ **Upload large amounts of data**: Uploading files and folders via the Web is a great way to get your files into the cloud (refer to the *Uploading files from your computer* section given in the book). But if you have a very large amount of data, you may find the sync program to be a faster and more convenient way of getting your files into Google Drive.

✦ **Keep files in sync with multiple computers**: You can install the Google Drive sync program on multiple computers and even mobile devices. This is a great way to propagate your files to multiple locations, which can be useful for productivity and work scenarios as well as for backup.

Using the Google Drive sync program is free, and it costs nothing to download or install. Files that you synchronize from your computer into Google Drive do count against your Google Drive storage space (just like any file you upload).

## Sync examples

Here are just a few ways you can use the Google Drive sync program.

✦ **Vacation photos**: Returning from vacation, you download the contents of your camera's memory card to your computer. But you want to share the vacation photos with your family. Simply move the folder of vacation photos over to the `Google Drive` folder, and they will automatically be uploaded to the cloud, into Google Drive. From there, you can share the folder, and others can then add their own photos from the vacation. Any photos other people add to your shared folder in the cloud will automatically sync to your own computer.

+ **Receiving a fax**: You install a third-party add-on faxing program for Google Drive. One of the features of this program is that you get a special phone number that you can use to receive faxes. When you receive a fax, the program automatically converts the fax to PDF format and puts the PDF file into a special `Received Faxes` folder in Google Drive. Immediately upon receiving the fax, the PDF created in the cloud will then be synced to all your devices where you can then view the PDF.

+ **Microsoft Office**: You are working on a document or presentation in Microsoft Office on your PC or Mac. You also want to be able to work on this file in the cloud when you may not have access to your computer. You keep the file in your `Google Drive` folder, and as you work on it, all the changes are kept in sync with Google Drive, so you always have access to the latest copy on the Web. You install a third-party add-on application that can edit Microsoft Office files in Google Drive, and you use this when you are travelling and away from your work or home computer. The changes you make to the file in Google Drive on the Web while on the road are saved and automatically synced to your computer, so when you get back from your trip, you're ready to keep working, picking up with the latest version right where you left off.

**Working with Microsoft Office files**

Although you can work with Microsoft Office files in the way described, it is often best to convert it to Google Docs format and work with that format instead. Refer to the *Context menu* section for how to convert files to Google Docs format. Working with the file in a Google Docs format is much easier, especially for editing and when you need to share the file with others.

## File syncing basics

When you install the Google Drive sync program on your computer, everything is kept up-to-date between the cloud (Google Drive on the Web) and your computer, automatically and in the background.

Only files kept in a special `Google Drive` folder on your computer's hard drive are uploaded and kept in sync.

When you install the sync program, any files that you have already in Google Drive on the Web will be downloaded and placed into the `Google Drive` folder on your hard drive. Any files that you move into this folder on your hard drive (for example, from your `Documents` folder) will be uploaded to Google Drive on the Web.

Here are the most important basics on how syncing works:

✦ When you create or upload files in Google Drive (on the Web at `https://drive.google.com`), they will be copied down to a special `Google Drive` folder on your computer's hard drive. On Windows, by default this folder will be located in `C:\Users\YourUserName\Google Drive`. On Mac, it will be in `/Users/YourUserName/Google Drive`.

✦ The same applies in the reverse direction when you create a file in the `Google Drive` folder on your computer's hard drive. It will be uploaded in the background to Google Drive on the Web, and you can then see the file in the cloud. If you have Google Drive installed on multiple computers (or on your mobile device), the files will sync back down to those devices, too.

✦ Similarly, if you make changes to existing files in Google Drive on the Web, those changes will sync to their counterparts in the `Google Drive` folder on your computer's hard drive. And as you would expect, changes made to a file in the `Google Drive` folder on your computer sync back up to Google Drive on the Web.

✦ Note that only files in the special `Google Drive` folder on your computer's hard drive are kept in sync on the Web. Files in other folders, for example files in your `Documents` or `My Documents` folder, will not be uploaded to the Web or kept in sync.

✦ For files on your computer that you want to upload and sync to the cloud (Google Drive on the Web), you will need to *move* them into the `Google Drive` folder on your computer's hard drive. You could do this using the *Cut* and *Paste* menu options, for example, which will move the file (not copy it). That way, you avoid making duplicate copies of files.

That's all there is to it. The key thing to know when using the Google Drive sync program is that your files are kept up-to-date everywhere, across all your devices, automatically.

The following diagram shows how it all works:

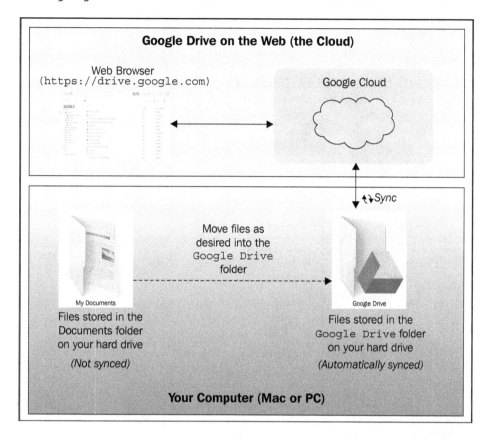

There are two main concepts here—the cloud, and your computer. When files are in the cloud (in Google Drive), you can access them with your web browser. When you install the Google Drive sync program, which is an add-on program (and not Google Drive itself), this program will monitor a special folder on your computer called `Google Drive`. Files you move into this special folder on your computer, for example out of your `Documents` folder, will be uploaded to the cloud by the sync program where you can then access them using a web browser. Files you create on the Web will also be copied into your computer's special `Google Drive` folder by the sync program.

## Downloading and installing Google Drive

Installing the Google Drive sync program, known also as Google Drive for PC or Mac, is done in a few simple steps:

1.  First, navigate your web browser to `https://drive.google.com`.

2.  Click on the **Download Google Drive** button, found at the bottom of the Navigation panel on the left-hand side of the screen:

3.  This will download the Google Drive installation file. For PC, the file will be called `googledrivesync.exe`; for Mac, the file will be called `installgoogledrive.dmg`.

4.  For PC, open the downloaded installation file to begin the installation process. For Mac, open the installation file, and then drag the Google Drive into your `Applications` folder. Installation of the sync program is quick (involving just a few prompts), and proceeding with the default options is just fine.

5.  You will be prompted to enter your Google account username and password for the account that you would like to keep in sync with your computer.

6.  Once installed, launch the program (Start menu for PC, `Applications` folder for Mac).

7.  Follow any of the remaining instructions to complete the installation.

That's it! Google Drive is now installed for your PC or Mac. Your files in Google Drive will now start syncing to your computer's hard drive. This happens continually while your computer is on. If you turn your computer off, no worries: the next time it boots back up, Google Drive will load automatically and then check for any changes that have been made on the Web, and update the files in your computer as needed.

## Working with the Google Drive sync program

As we've seen, syncing files with the Google Drive sync program is automatic. File syncing is done in the background, with syncing done within seconds of a change either on your computer or the Web.

Installing Google Drive on your PC or Mac creates a special folder on your computer's hard drive called `Google Drive`. It's similar to other folders on your hard drive, with one difference: files and folders that you move into this folder on your computer will get uploaded and kept in sync with Google Drive on the Web.

The general idea is to move any files on your computer that you want to back up or keep in sync from their original folder (for example, `Documents`) into this special `Google Drive` folder. Note that it's best to *move* files into the `Google Drive` folder, not *copy* them. Otherwise, you'll have copies of the file in two different places (which can be problematic when you make changes).

To get started, open the special `Google Drive` folder on your computer by clicking on the **Open Google Drive** folder in the menu that appears when you click on the Google Drive icon. For Windows, the icon appears in the system tray in the bottom-right corner of the screen:

On a Mac, the icon is on the menu bar in the upper-right corner of the screen:

If you had files already in Google Drive, you will see that they are in the process of being synced to the `Google Drive` folder on your computer. Files are synced one by one so you will gradually see them appear in the folder. If you have a large number of files to sync, this could take several minutes, hours, or more.

To get the current sync status, open the Google Drive menu by clicking on the Google Drive icon in the taskbar. The first item that appears will be the synchronization status, which will indicate that the sync is complete, or if the sync is not complete, then the current sync progress will be displayed:

At this point, there's nothing more you need to do. Everything is automatic. If you'd like to upload and keep the files on your computer in sync with Google Drive, simply move them into the `Google Drive` folder. To stop syncing them, move them out of the `Google Drive` folder on your hard drive, and they will no longer be kept in sync or be available in Google Drive on the Web.

Just like with uploading files through the Web, note that files that are uploaded to and kept in sync with Google Drive on the Web using the sync program will count against your storage space in Google Drive, just as if you had uploaded them through the Web. In other words, files in Google Drive on the Web—whether they got there from the sync program, or from being uploaded manually—take up space in Google Drive.

## Choosing which folders to sync

By default, all folders in Google Drive will be synced. However, you have the option of only syncing some folders of your choosing. To set this preference:

1. Open the Google Drive menu by clicking on the Google Drive icon, and then choose **Preferences**. The **Preferences** screen will appear.

2. Under the **Sync** options section, check the **Only sync some folders to this computer** checkbox.

3. You should see all of the folders in Google Drive in the list, each with a checkbox.

4. Check the ones you want to sync, and leave the ones you don't want synced unchecked.

5. Click on the **Apply changes** button, and your selections will be recorded.

# 7 – Using Google Drive on your phone or tablet

You can access your files on the go from your mobile device using the Google Drive app for Android (phone and tablet) or for iOS (iPhone and iPad). Using these free apps, you can download, view, and even edit your files right on your device. You can even upload photos you take with your phone right into Google Drive. All the other features you're used to using on the Web work just as you'd expect on your phone or tablet including searching, sorting, sharing, and organizing.

## Installing the Google Drive app for Android

The Google Drive app for Android is available for free from the Google Play Store, and it supports both phones and tablets.

To install the app, visit the Google Play Store by tapping the Play Store icon on your Android device. Find the application called **Google Drive** (you can search for it), and then install the app. Note you can also install the app by visiting Google's Play Store on the Web at `https://play.google.com`. Once installed, launch the app by tapping the Google Drive app icon in your device's apps screen.

## Installing the Google Drive App for iPhone or iPad

The Google Drive app for iPhone and iPad is available for free from Apple's App Store, and it supports both phones and tablets.

To install the app, visit the App Store by taping on the App Store icon on your iPhone or iPad. Find the application called **Google Drive** (you can search for it), and then install the app. Once installed, launch the app by tapping on the Google Drive app icon in your device's apps screen.

## Using the Mobile App

For Android, iPhone, and iPad, the various flavors of the mobile Google Drive app all have the same basic functionality and work in similar ways. In fact, you'll recognize many of the basic user interface pieces from earlier in this book.

## Navigation panel

This corresponds to the Navigation panel on Google Drive for the Web, and functions in the exact same way. Tapping an item in this panel will update the files shown in the Files list on your mobile device.

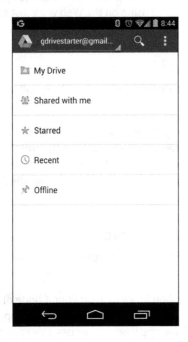 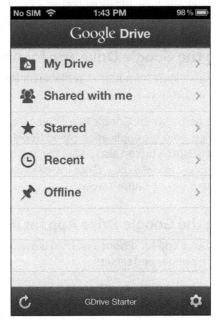

The labels correspond to those found in the Navigation panel on Google Drive for the Web:

✦ **My Drive** is where all files that you've created appear. Note that, unlike on the Web, your hierarchy of folders is not shown; instead, folders will be shown in the Files list and you can "drill down" into them as needed.

✦ **Shared with me** is where all files that other people have shared with you appear. Clicking on this will filter your Files list to only those items.

✦ **Starred** will show only those files that you have previously starred.

✦ **Recent** shows a list of files sorted by modification date; use this to quickly find files that have most recently been created or edited by you or someone else.

✦ **Offline** will show a list of files that are available for viewing offline, that is, while not connected to the Internet. Files can be marked to be kept offline in the Preview panel, discussed later.

# Files list

The Files list appears when you tap on any of the items in the Navigation panel; for tablet devices that have a larger screen, the list will simply always be present to the right-hand side of the Navigation panel. In this example, we are in the **Family** folder.

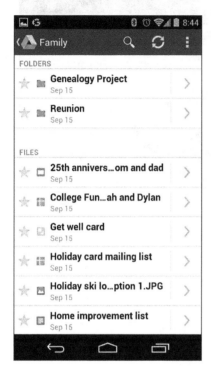
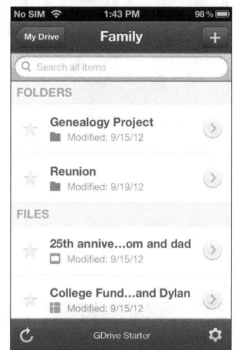

For each file in this list, you can:

✦ See the file's title, icon, and the date that the file was last modified.

✦ Tap on the star to toggle whether the file is *starred*.

✦ Tap on the arrow on the right-hand side to get additional details about the file via the Preview panel.

✦ Tap on a file to open it. Google types can be previewed and even edited on the device. If you have an app installed on your device that can open the file, such as a PDF viewer or image editor, you'll have the opportunity to use that app to view the file.

## Preview panel

The Preview panel shows a visual preview and additional details about the file, and also permits you to take additional actions on the file.

From the Preview panel, you can:

✦ See the icon and title of the file

✦ See a thumbnail (small image) preview of the file

✦ Open the file by tapping on the **Open** button or the file thumbnail

✦ See with whom a file is shared and their level of access (view or edit)

✦ Share the file with other people

✦ Mark the file as **Available offline** which means it will be copied onto your device and is viewable on the device even when you don't have an Internet connection

✦ Return to the Files list by closing the Preview panel

## Actions menu

The **Actions** menu lets you perform certain operations on the selected file. It is very similar to the Context menu that appears in Google Drive for the Web. To pop open the **Actions** menu in Android, long-press (tap-and-hold) a file in the Files list. For iPhone/iPad, click on the "Actions" icon in the upper-right corner of the Preview panel.

Here are some of the things you can do in the **Actions** menu:

✦ **Share** the file with one or more people

✦ **Rename** the file

✦ **Move** the file to a different folder in Google Drive

✦ **Remove** the file, placing it in the Trash

✦ **Print** the file to any printer using Google Cloud Print

✦ **Send** the file via e-mail

Depending on the application version, certain other advanced options, such as printing, may be supported.

## Create menu

The Create menu (or **Add** menu on iPhone/iPad) lets you create new items in Google Drive directly from your phone. This menu appears by clicking on the menu icon in the toolbar and selecting **New**, or by clicking on the **+** icon in the toolbar on iPhone/iPad.

From the Create menu, you can create a new Google Docs document, a new folder, or you can upload a photo or video from your phone directly into Google Drive.

## Searching for files

Just like with Google Drive on the Web, you can quickly search all of your files in Google Drive. On Android, click on the search icon in the toolbar which will display the search box (this is always visible on iPhone/iPad), and type in your query. Files matching your search will appear in the Files list. From here, you can work with a matching search result like any other file: open, preview, star, share, and more.

## Access your files and create new ones, wherever you are!

You can see that the mobile experience for Google Drive is robust and full-featured. With the Google Drive mobile app, you can do the majority of the same things you can with a web browser on your desktop—viewing, editing, and sharing on the go.

# People and places you should get to know

If you need help with Google Drive, or just want to learn more about Google Drive in general, here are some people and places that will prove invaluable.

## Official sites for Google Drive

+ **Main page**: To work with your files on the Web using Google Drive go to
  `https://drive.google.com`

+ **Start guide**: For getting started with Google Drive, including sign-up information
  visit `https://drive.google.com/start`

+ **Help Center**: To browse an extensive set of Google-authored help pages about
  Google Drive and covering all aspects of the product go to `https://support.google.com/drive`

+ **Google Apps for Business**: For helpful information on how to use Google Drive and
  other Google Apps in the workplace visit `https://www.google.com/intl/en/enterprise/apps/business/`

+ **Google Apps for Education**: For helpful information on how to use Google Drive
  and other Google Apps in your school or university visit `https://www.google.com/intl/en/enterprise/apps/education/`

## Articles and tutorials

+ **How to set up 2-factor verification**: To ensure your Google Account stays as
  secure as possible go to `https://support.google.com/accounts/bin/topic.py?topic=28786`

+ **Google Drive overview**: For an overview by Wall Street Journal's Walt Mossberg
  watch `https://www.youtube.com/watch?v=AzrixPhql54`

+ **How to share**: To learn more on how to share in Google Drive visit
  `https://support.google.com/drive/bin/answer.py?answer=2494822`

+ **Techniques for searching**: For more on searching techniques in Google Drive go
  to `https://support.google.com/drive/bin/answer.py?answer=2375114`

## Community

+ **User community**: To browse official product forums where you can ask Google
  employees and other experts specific questions about Google Drive, go to
  `https://productforums.google.com/forum/#!forum/drive`

+ **Google+ page**: For tips, tutorials, announcements, and community discussion
  go to `https://plus.google.com/+GoogleDrive`

+ **Twitter page**: For frequent short updates and tips visit `https://twitter.com/GoogleDriveNews`

## Blogs

✦ **Google Drive blog**: For announcements related to Google Drive go to
`https://googledrive.blogspot.com`

✦ **Official Google blog**: For all major Google-related announcements see
`https://googleblog.blogspot.com`

Thank you for buying
# Instant Google Drive Starter

## About Packt Publishing

Packt, pronounced 'packed', published its first book "*Mastering phpMyAdmin for Effective MySQL Management*" in April 2004 and subsequently continued to specialize in publishing highly focused books on specific technologies and solutions.

Our books and publications share the experiences of your fellow IT professionals in adapting and customizing today's systems, applications, and frameworks. Our solution based books give you the knowledge and power to customize the software and technologies you're using to get the job done. Packt books are more specific and less general than the IT books you have seen in the past. Our unique business model allows us to bring you more focused information, giving you more of what you need to know, and less of what you don't.

Packt is a modern, yet unique publishing company, which focuses on producing quality, cutting-edge books for communities of developers, administrators, and newbies alike. For more information, please visit our website: www.packtpub.com.

## Writing for Packt

We welcome all inquiries from people who are interested in authoring. Book proposals should be sent to author@packtpub.com. If your book idea is still at an early stage and you would like to discuss it first before writing a formal book proposal, contact us; one of our commissioning editors will get in touch with you.

We're not just looking for published authors; if you have strong technical skills but no writing experience, our experienced editors can help you develop a writing career, or simply get some additional reward for your expertise.

## Ext GWT 2.0: Beginner's Guide

ISBN: 978-1-84951-184-1          Paperback: 320 pages

Take the user experience of your website to a new level
with Ext GWT

1. Explore the full range of features of the Ext GWT
   library through practical, step-by-step examples

2. Discover how to combine simple building blocks
   into powerful components

3. Create powerful Rich Internet Applications
   with features normally only found in desktop
   applications

## Google App Inventor: Beginner's Guide

ISBN: 978-1-84969-212-0          Paperback: 356 pages

Create powerful Android apps the easy all-visual way with
Google App Inventor

1. All the basics of App Inventor in plain English with
   lots of illustrations

2. Learn how apps get created with lots of simple, fun
   examples

3. By an author with over 100 books, who keeps it
   entertaining, informative, and memorable. You'll be
   inventing apps from the first day.

Please check **www.packtpub.com** for information on our titles

## Google Visualization API Essentials

ISBN: 978-1-84969-436-0      Paperback: 274 pages

Make sense of your data: make it visual with the Google Visualization API

1. Wrangle all sorts of data into a visual format, without being an expert programmer

2. Visualize new or existing spreadsheet data through charts, graphs, and maps

3. Full of diagrams, core concept explanations, best practice tips, and links to working book examples

## Google SketchUp for Game Design: Beginner's Guide

ISBN: 978-1-84969-134-5      Paperback: 270 pages

Create 3D game worlds complete with textures, levels, and props

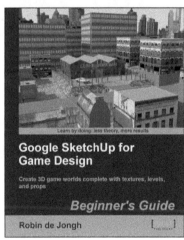

1. Learn how to create realistic game worlds with Google's easy 3D modeling tool

2. Populate your games with realistic terrain, buildings, vehicles, and objects

3. Import to game engines such as Unity 3D and create a first person 3D game simulation

4. Learn the skills you need to sell low polygon 3D objects in game asset stores

Please check **www.packtpub.com** for information on our titles